OVERCOMING THE MEMORIES OF DIVORCE

"Thus saith the Lord, Where is the bill of your mother's divorcement, whom I have put away?"

Isaiah50:1

By
Franklin N. Abazie

Overcoming the Memories of Divorce

COPYRIGHT 2018 BY Franklin N Abazie
ISBN: 978-1-945-133-5-10
All right reserved. This book or any portion thereof may not be reproduced or used in any manner whatsoever without the express written permission of the publisher, except for the use of brief quotations in a book review. All Bible quotes are from King James Version and others as noted.

Published by: F N ABAZIE PUBLISHING HOUSE---
a.k.a,
Empowerment Bookstore:

That I may publish with the voice of thanksgiving and tell of all thy wondrous works. **Psalms 26:7**

To order additional copies, wholesales or booking: Call the Church office (973-372-7518)
or Empowerment Bookstore Hotline 973-393-8518
Worship address:
343 Sanford Avenue Newark New Jersey 07106
Administrative Head Office address:
33 Schley Street Newark New Jersey 07112
Email: pastorfranknto@yahoo.com
Website www.fnabaziehealingministries.org
Publishing House: www.fnabaziepublishinghouse.org

This book is a production of F N Abazie Publishing House.

A publication Arms of Miracle of God Ministries 2018
First Edition

CONTENTS

THE MANDATE OF THE COMMISSION...........iv

ARMS OF THE COMMISSION............................v

INTRODUCTION...viii

CHAPTER 1

1. Living in Denial of Your Divorce 28

CHAPTER 2

2. Rebuilding life After Divorce...........................53

CHAPTER 3

3. Prayer of Salvation..74

CHAPTER 4

4. About the Author...82

THE MANDATE OF THE COMMISSION

"THE MOMENT IS DUE TO IMPACT YOUR WORLD THROUGH THE REVIVAL OF THE HEALING & MIRACLE MINISTRY OF JESUS CHRIST OF NAZARETH.

I AM SENDING YOU TO RESTORE HEALTH UNTO THEE AND I WILL HEAL THEE OF THY WOUNDS, SAID THE LORD OF HOST."

ARMS OF THE COMMISSION

1) F N Abazie Ministries-Miracle of God Ministries (Miracle Chapel Intl)

2) F N Abazie TV Ministries: Global Television Ministry Outreach.

3) F N Abazie Radio Ministries: Radio Broadcasting Outreach.

4) F N Abazie Publishing House: Book Publication.

5) F N Abazie Bible School: also called Word of Healing Bible School (W.O.H.B.S)

6) F N Abazie Evangelistic Ass: Miracle of God Ministries: Global Crusade

7) Empowerment Bookstore: Book distribution.

8) F N Abazie Helping Hands: Meeting the help of the needy world wide

9) F N Abazie Disaster Recovery Mission: Global Disaster Recovery.

10) F N Abazie Prison Ministry: Prison Ministry for all convicts "Second chance"

Some of our ministry arms are waiting the appointed time to commence

FAVOR CONFESSION

Father thank you for making me righteous and accepted through the blood of Jesus Christ. Because of that, I am blessed and highly favored by God. I am the subject of your affection. Your favor surrounds me as a shield, and the first thing that people see around me is your favored shield.

Thank you that I have favor with you and man today. All day long people go out of their way to bless me and help me. I have favor with everyone that I deal with today. Doors that were once closed are now opened for me. I receive preferential treatment, and I have special privileges, I am Gods favored child.

No good thing will he withhold from me. Because of Gods favor my enemies cannot triumph over my life. I have supernatural increase and promotion. I declare restoration to everything that the devil has stolen from my life. I have honor in the midst of my adversaries and an increase in assets, especially in real estate and expansion of territories.

Because I am highly favored by God, I experience great victories, supernatural turnarounds, and miraculous breakthrough in the midst of great impossibilities. I receive recognition, prominence, and honor. Petitions are granted to me even by ungodly authorities. Policies, rules, regulations, and laws are changed and reverse on my behalf.

I win battles that I don't even have to fight, because God fights them for me. This is the day, the set time and the designated moment for me to experience the free favor of God, that profusely and lavishly abound on my behalf in Jesus name. Amen.

INTRODUCTION

"For the Lord, the God of Israel, saith that he hateth putting away: for one covereth violence with his garment, saith the Lord of hosts." **Mal2:16**

I may never get the chance to meet you in person, but this literature has given me the chance to meet you. *Overcoming the memories of Divorce* is a book compiled by the Holy Spirit as a result of prevailing counselling sessions with some active parishioners who became *victims of denial of divorce*.

"For this cause shall a man leave his father and mother, and cleave to his wife." **Mark10:7**.

The bible says that the only reason a man should leave his father house to cleave to his wife is because of marriage. The truth is most of us men refused to leave our father's house to cleave with our wife. If there is no agreement and no communication, there is no union.

The word of God says, *"And they twain shall be one flesh: so then they are no more twain, but one flesh."* **Mark10:8**

By the help of the Holy Spirit, we have tried to explain a few primary objective and common goal for any marriage to last before God.

We are told *"What therefore God hath joined together, let not man put asunder."* **Mark10:9**

As a strong advocate of divorce, I believe this small book will go a long way to answers some complex issues of marriage. God hates divorce. "For I hate divorce," says the Lord, the God of Israel. You can have the best of life. You can enjoy marriage again. Open your eyes and allow the Holy Spirit to mold your heart in Jesus Name.

Happy Reading!

HIS DESTINY WAS THE CROSS….

HIS PURPOSE WAS LOVE…..

HIS REASON WAS YOU….

"Thus saith the Lord, Where is the bill of your mother's divorcement, whom I have put away?"

Isaiah50:1

"For the Lord, the God of Israel, saith that he hateth putting away: for one covereth violence with his garment, saith the Lord of hosts: therefore take heed to your spirit, that ye deal not treacherously."

Mal2:16

"For this cause shall a man leave his father and mother, and cleave to his wife."

Mark10:7

"And they twain shall be one flesh: so then they are no more twain, but one flesh."

Mark10:8

"What therefore God hath joined together, let not man put asunder."

Mark10:9

Prayer Points

"If ye shall ask any thing in my name, I will do it.." **John14:14**

Holy Spirit of God frustrate and disappoint, every one that is against my life and family, in the name of Jesus.

Father Lord destroy every demonic networks and traps against my progress in life in the name of Jesus.

Fire of God, destroy every demonic projection and curses against my life and destiny in the name of Jesus.

Every spell and curses pronounced against my destiny, break, in the name of Jesus.

Hand of God cage every power militating against my rising in life, in the name of Jesus.

Power of God silent every voice raising a counter motion against my elevation, in the mighty name of Jesus.

Blood of Jesus neutralize every spirit of Balaam hired to hinder my life, ministry, and career, the name of Jesus.

Fire of God destroy every curse that I have brought into my life through ignorance and disobedience, break by fire, in the name of Jesus.

Ancient of day destroy every power harassing my ministry in the name of Jesus.

Father God deliver me from invincible forces militating against my life and destiny.

Power of God frustrate every coven and demonic network, designed to frustrate and hinder my success in life, in the name of Jesus.

I dismantle every strong hold designed to imprison my talent in the mighty name of Jesus.

I reject every cycle of frustration, in the name of Jesus.

Power of God paralyze every agent assigned to frustrate my life in the name of Jesus.

Finger of God, grant me supernatural speed against all my contenders in the name of Jesus.

By the blood of Jesus, I destroy every familiar spirit caging my life and career.

Fire of God arrest every demonic agents, assigned to police my destiny and marriage.

By the blood of Jesus, I proclaim no weapon fashioned against me shall ever prosper.

Holy Spirit of God break me through and forward in life in the mighty name of Jesus.

God, smash me and renew my strength, in the name of Jesus.

Holy Spirit, open my eyes to see beyond the visible to the invisible, in the name of Jesus.

Father Lord grant me strength and power in the name of Jesus.

O Lord, liberate my spirit to follow the leading of the Holy Spirit.

Holy Spirit, teach me to pray through problems instead of praying about, it in the name of Jesus.

Father Lord, deliver me from the false accusation in life, in the name of Jesus.

By the blood of Jesus, every evil spiritual padlock and evil chain hindering my success, be roasted, in the name of Jesus.

By the blood of Jesus I rebuke every spirit of spiritual deafness and blindness in my life, in the name of Jesus.

Father Lord, empower me to dominate the enemy of my destiny in the name of Jesus.

Jesus Christ of Nazareth, heal my infirmities in the name of Jesus.

Lord, anoint my eyes and my ears that they may see and hear wondrous things from heaven.

Father Lord, anoint me with power and authority to dominate all my enemies in the name of Jesus.

Fire of God roast every giant rising up against my life and career.

Holy Spirit of God destroy all my oppressors in the name of Jesus.

Angels of good new, bring my good news to me in the mighty name of Jesus.

Every strong man holding me down, lose your hold now in the name of Jesus.

I nullify every demonic prediction over my life in the name of Jesus.

By the blood of Jesus, I flush out every polluted deposit of the enemy in my life.

By the blood of Jesus, I paralyze every enemy of my promotion in the name of Jesus.

Father Lord, destroy any power tormenting my life that is not from you.

Holy Ghost fire, ignite the fire of revival in my life.

By the blood of Jesus, I declare victory over every conflicting trial.

By the Blood of Jesus, I command the arrest of every demonic spirit, militating against my life .

By the blood of Jesus, I proclaimed the blood of Jesus, over every device of the enemy.

By the blood of Jesus, I revoke stagnation and hardship over my life in the name of Jesus.

Holy Ghost fire, destroy every satanic arrangement in my life, in the name of Jesus.

Circular problems, assigned to my life, you will not prosper, backfire, in the name of Jesus.

Every satanic project, against my breakthrough, explode in the face of the enemy, in the name of Jesus.

Every dream of backwardness, go back to your senders, in the name of Jesus.

Any power, working round the clock, with dark powers, against my life, perish, in the name of Jesus.

Every household Cain, assigned to waste my Abel, you will not succeed, rush to your grave and die, in the name of Jesus.

Every domestic enemy, anointed by Satan, to terminate my life, terminate your own life, in the name of Jesus.

Anti-Christ power of my father's house, assigned to punish me, die, in the name of Jesus.

Every satanic contact of my father's house, hunting for my life, die, in the name of Jesus.

Every magician, astrologer and diviner, assigned against me, go back to your senders, in the name of Jesus.

Every evil progress, against my life, perish, in the name of Jesus.

Mid-night and mid-day arrows, fired at me, collide on the Rock of Ages and backfire, in the name of Jesus.

Every giant, occupying my promised land, lose your hold, in the name of Jesus.

By the power that silenced Sennacherib, I silence my adversaries forever, in the name of Jesus.

Every wicked altar, harboring my name and my picture, collide with thunder and die, in the name of Jesus.

Every affliction, targeted at me, explode in the hands of your owners, in the name of Jesus.

Every king Saul of my household, pursuing my David, die, in the name of Jesus

Satanic grave digger of my father's house, dig your own grave and enter into it, in the name of Jesus.

Any power that has joined witchcraft and occult group to attack me, thus saith the Lord, suffer not a witch to live, lose your life for my sake, in the name of Jesus.

Arrows of shame, disgrace, and mockery, fired into my life, backfire, in the name of Jesus.

Arrows of rise and fall, fired at me, expire, in the name of Jesus.

Every vulture of darkness, assigned to eat my flesh, go back to your senders, in the name of Jesus.

Every verdict of darkness, issued against me, backfire, in the name of Jesus.

Every dominant wicked power of my father's house, I bury you now, in the name of Jesus.

Every satanic traditional manipulation, assigned to remove my glory, fail, in the name of Jesus.

Any power, assigned to make me irrelevant in my generation, your time is up, die, in the name of Jesus.

Any power, giving me a deadline to die, fall down, and die on your own deadline, in the name of Jesus.

Every strange material and strange deposit, in my body, disappear now and go back to your senders, in the name of Jesus.

Every satanic payroll, where my enemies registered my name, I delete my name and substitute it with the names of the enemies, in the name of Jesus.

Any wicked hand, collecting evil against me, decay, and die, in the name of Jesus.

By the power that silenced Haman in favor of Mordecai, O Lord, let every power assigned against my existence, die, in the name of Jesus.

Any power assigned to manipulate my destiny, enough is enough, scatter, in the name of Jesus.

Every assembly of the wicked, delegated to destroy my destiny, scatter, in the name of Jesus.

Every ancient strongman, laboring to waste my efforts, my life is not your victim, expire, in the name of Jesus.

Every wicked mouth, sowing evil seeds against me, I command the seeds to catch fire, in the name of Jesus.

Every ancient gate, standing against my breakthroughs, scatter, in the name of Jesus.

I plug my destiny, into the mystery of divine favor, in the name of Jesus.

O thou that troubled the Israel of Miracles of God Ministries, the God of Elijah shall trouble you today.

Every enemy, of the Miracles of God Ministries, scatter, in the name of Jesus.

O God, arise and uproot anything You did not plant inside the Miracles of God Ministries, in Jesus' name.

You fire of revival, fall upon Miracles of God Ministries, in the name of Jesus.

CHAPTER 1
Living in Denial of your Divorce

Often some of us who are divorced a long time ago, live in denial of that divorce. The truth is that you are living in denial of that same *divorce*. You are now alone in the physical but your *emotions, spirit, soul, and body*, is still attached to that relationship. Often our memory replays the events that brings back full remembrance of all that took place in that marriage. Indeed going through a divorce in life can be very catastrophic.

It is one of the most difficult challenges of the brain-to adjust to it. Often our memory bank replays almost all the events that unfolded in the marriage, both good and bad. Divorce has power to affect our destiny, it can turn our life upside down for the worst or for good.

It is written, *"And they twain shall be one flesh: so then they are no more twain, but one flesh."* **Mark10:7**

"And said, For this cause shall a man leave father and mother, and shall cleave to his wife: and they twain shall be one flesh? Wherefore they are no more twain, but one flesh. What therefore God hath joined together, let not man put asunder." **Mathew 19:5-6**

Divorce is an emotional task therefore most people react to it differently. Although some people do well and move on with their lives after divorce. A greater percentage of people are emotionally tied to their marriage even after divorce. The power of *soul tie and retained memory has power to make us live in denial of the divorce.*

While some individuals move on with their lives well after divorce, others are stuck and live in denial of the divorce of that marriage. To maneuver through the challenges of life after divorce, we need persistent prayer unto God to have mercy.

Chapter 1 - Living in Denial of your Divorce

THE CONSEQUENCES OF DIVORCE

It is fair enough to be sad when the marriage comes to an end. But we must not remain sad for the rest of our lives. Although those memories are painful, grief is a healthy emotional response to the loss of a significant relationship.

It is written,

"For this cause shall a man leave his father and mother, and cleave to his wife." **Mark10:7**

"And they twain shall be one flesh: so then they are no more twain, but one flesh." **Mark10:8**

"What therefore God hath joined together, let not man put asunder." **Mark10:9**

Although sorrow and grief can be very complex to handle, most people do understand and accept the inevitability of these feelings. Living in denial is the worst thing anyone can do to themselves in life. It has power to paralyze our entire future.

Living in denial can make anyone fall into depression-this is simply because of the overwhelming negative feeling of failure, shame, and disappointment.

Often we know a lot of folks around us who have experienced these feelings. People who feel overwhelmed and confused in this way tend to fall back upon old habits of thought and action rather than looking intelligently at the facts of their situation and weighing the best choices for the future. As long as *you live in denial, you will never be able to create a great future for your life*.

The after effect of divorce is so complicated that it has power to control anyone who is a victim. Generally, people tend to focus on the worst-case, or best-case scenarios whenever they imagine the final divorce decree from the judge.

The assumption that life after divorce is gratifying depends on the individual. There are numerous of stories of men who quickly move on to new, happier relationships and women who feel liberated upon divorcing.

Chapter 1 - Living in Denial of your Divorce

The decision to end a relationship is very traumatic, chaotic, and filled with contradictory emotions. There are also specific feelings, attitudes, and dynamics associated with whether one is in the role of the initiator or the receiver of the decision to breakup.

For example, it is not unusual for the *initiator to experience fear, relief, distance, impatience, resentment, doubt, and guilt.*

Likewise, when a party has not initiated the divorce, they may feel shock, betrayal, loss of control, victimization, decreased self-esteem, insecurity, anger, a desire to *"get even"* and wishes to reconcile.

To normalize most people's experiences during this time, it may be helpful to know that typical emotional stages have been identified with ending a relationship. It may also be helpful to understand that marriages do not breakdown overnight; the breakup is not the result of one incident; nor is the breakup the entire fault of one party.

The emotional breaking up process typically extends over several years and is confounded by each party being at different stages in the emotional process while in the same stage of the physical (or legal) process.

It is also quite normal to do different things to try to create distance from the former partner while divorcing. Unfortunately, this distancing often takes the form of fault finding. Not to be disrespectful, but it's not unlike the process one goes through in deciding to buy a new car: somehow every flaw in that favorite old car needs to be noticed and exaggerated in order to feel okay about selling it.

Also, if the other person is portrayed as really awful, one can escape any responsibility for the end of the marriage. A common response to divorce is to seek vengeance. When parties put their focus on getting even, there is an equal amount of energy expended on being blameless. What's true is that blaming and fault finding are not necessary or really helpful.

Chapter 1 - Living in Denial of your Divorce

Another normal rationalization is that the marriage was a wholly unpleasant experience and escaping it is good. Or the marriage was unpleasant and now the other partner must make this up in the divorce. Thinking that the marriage was wholly unpleasant is unfair to both parties and can hinder emotional healing.

Both stayed in the marriage for as long as they did because there were some good things about it. There were also some things that did not work for them and these are why they are divorcing.

Much of your healing will involve acceptance, focusing on the future, taking responsibility for their own actions (now and during the marriage, and after the divorce), and acting with integrity.

Focusing on the future they would like to create may require an acknowledgment of each other's differing emotional stages and a compassionate willingness to work together to balance the emotional comfort of both parties.

The following information on the emotional stages of ending a relationship is provided to help parties through the emotional quagmire of ending a relationship and assist in their personal healing.

I. DISILLUSIONMENT OF ONE PARTY
(sometimes 1-2 years before verbalized)

A. Vague feelings of discontentment, arguments, stored resentments, breaches of trust.

B. Problems are real but unacknowledged

C. Greater distance; lack of mutuality

D. Confidential, fantasy, consideration of pros and cons of divorce

E. Development of strategy for separation

F. Feelings: fear, denial, anxiety, guilt, love, anger, depression, grief

Chapter 1 - Living in Denial of your Divorce

II. EXPRESSING DISSATISFACTION
(8-12 months before invoking legal process)

A. Expressing discontent or ambivalence to other party

B. Marital counseling, or

C. Possible honeymoon phase *(one last try)*

D. Feelings: relief *(that it's out in the open)*, tension, emotional roller coaster, guilt, anguish, doubt, grief

III. DECIDING TO DIVORCE
(6-12 months before invoking legal process)

A. Creating emotional distance *(i.e., disparaging the other person/situation in order to leave it)*

B. Seldom reversible *(because it's been considered for a while)*

C. Likely for an affair to occur

II. EXPRESSING DISSATISFACTION
(8-12 months before invoking legal process)

A.   Expressing discontent or ambivalence to other party

D.   Other person just begins Stage I *(considering divorce)* and feels denial, depressed, rejected, low self-esteem, anger

E.   Both parties feel victimized by the other

F.   Feelings: anger, resentment, sadness, guilt, anxiety for the family, the future, impatience with other, needy

IV. ACTING ON DECISION
(beginning the legal process)

A.   Physical separation

B.   Emotional separation *(complicated by emotional flare-ups)*

C.   Creating redefinition *(self-orientation)*

D.   Going public with the decision

Chapter 1 - Living in Denial of your Divorce

E. Setting the tone for the divorce process *(getting legal advice and setting legal precedent: children, support, home)*

F. Choosing sides and divided loyalties of friends and families

G. Usually when the children find out *(they may feel responsible, behave in ways to make parents interact)*

H. Feelings: traumatized, panic, fear, shame, guilt, blame, histrionics

V. GROWING ACCEPTANCE
(during the legal process or after)

A. Adjustments: physical, emotional

B. Accepting that the marriage wasn't happy or fulfilling

C. Regaining a sense of power and control, creating a plan for the future, creating a new identity, discovering new talents and resources

E. Setting the tone for the divorce process *(getting legal advice and setting legal precedent: children, support, home)*

D. This is the best time to be in mediation: parties can look forward and plan for the future; moods can be more elevated (thrill of a second chance at life)

VI. NEW BEGINNINGS
(completing the legal process to four years after)

A. Parties have moved beyond the blame and anger to forgiveness, new respect, and new roles

B. Experiences: insight, acceptance, integrity. Comparing Mediation and Litigation

Chapter 1 - Living in Denial of your Divorce

Why is mediation a compassionate and appropriate venue for helping people in divorce?

On the average, it takes family members approximately four to eight years to recover from the emotional and financial expense of a bitter adversarial divorce. In an adversarial divorce, there is no possible resolution of the emotional issues, only decreased trust and increased resentment.

A litigated divorce can cost each party $5,000 to $35,000. The focus is on assigning blame and fault and skirmishing for the most powerful position *(changing locks, freezing bank accounts, getting temporary custody of the children)*.

Communications between parties break down. Negotiations proceed through attorneys and are strategic and positioned. Attorneys have an ethical responsibility to zealously advocate for the best interest of their client.

Often there is no consideration of the best interests of the children or recognition for the need for parties to have an ongoing relationship because they have children, friends, extended family, and community together.

Going to court is an expensive risk; someone who does not know you makes decisions for you that will affect your whole life.

Mediators may save clients thousands of dollars in immediate and future legal and counseling fees. Mediators can focus parties on creating their best possible future and help parties resolve their emotional issues for the best interests of their children and their own psychological wellbeing.

Mediators can help parties feel understood, accept responsibility for the failure of the marriage, and, when there are children, begin to reshape their relationship from one of partners to co-parents.

Chapter 1 - Living in Denial of your Divorce

Mediators can empower clients by helping them be at their best *(rather than their worst)* during a challenging time in their lives, enable them to have an active role in their separating *(creative choice vs. court imposition)*, create a clear and understandable road map for the future, make informed decisions, and to look back at their behavior in the mediation of their divorce with integrity and self-respect.

Typical Reactions of Children to Divorce

Much of children's post-divorce adjustment is dependent on (1) the quality of their relationship with each parent before the divorce, (2) the intensity, and duration of the parental conflict, and (3) the parents' ability to focus on the needs of the children in the divorce.

Typically, children whose parents are going through a rough divorce engage in behaviors which are designed to help them feel secure. What follows are some typical experiences of children to divorce and separation:

A. DENIAL

This especially occurs in young children and surfaces as storytelling (Mommy and Daddy and me going to Disneyland; we're moving into a duplex and Daddy will live next door; they will also have reconciliation fantasies).

B. ABANDONMENT

When parents separate, children worry who will take care of them. They are afraid they too are divorceable and will be abandoned by one or both of their parents. This problem is worsened by one or both parents taking the children into their confidence, talking about the other parent in front of the children, using language like "Daddy is divorcing us," being late for pick-up, or abducting the children.

Children who are feeling insecure will say things to a parent which is intended to evoke a mama bear/papa bear response (a demonstration of protectiveness).

Chapter 1 - Living in Denial of your Divorce

If children do not have "permission" to have a good relationship with the other parent, or if they think they need to "take care of" one of their parents in the divorce, they are likely to end up having feelings of divided loyalties between their parents or, in the extreme, they may become triangulated with one parent against the other parent.

C. PREOCCUPATION WITH INFORMATION

Children will want details of what is happening and how it affects them. Communication from the parents needs to be unified and age appropriate.

D. ANGER AND HOSTILITY

Children may express anger and hostility with peers, siblings, or parents. School performance may be impaired. Hostility of children toward parents is often directed at the parent perceived to be at fault. Hostility turned inward looks like depression in children.

E. DEPRESSION

Lethargy, sleep and eating disturbances, acting out, social withdrawal, physical injury *(more common in adolescents)*.

F. IMMATURITY/HYPERMATURITY

Children may regress to an earlier developmental stage when they felt assured of both parents' love. They may do some "baby-talk" or wet their beds. Children may become "parentified" by what they perceive to be the emotional and physical needs of their parents *("Someone needs to be in charge here.")*

G. PREOCCUPATION WITH RECONCILIATION

The more conflict there is between the parents, the longer children hold onto the notion of their parents' reconciliation. It is clear that the parents are not "getting on" with their lives. Children will often act out in ways which force their parents to interact *(negatively or positively)*.

Children whose parents were very conflictual during the marriage often mistake the strong emotions of conflict with intimacy. They see the parents as engaged in an intimate relationship.

H. BLAME AND GUILT

Because so much marital conflict may be related to the stress of parenting, children often feel responsible for their parents' divorce--they feel that somehow their behavior contributed to it. This is especially true when parents fight during exchanges of the children or in negotiating schedules: children see that parents are fighting over them. They may try to bargain their parents back together by promises of good behavior; they may have difficulty with transitions or refuse to go with the other parent.

I. ACTING OUT

Children will often act out their own and their parents' anger. In an attempt to survive in a hostile environment, children will often take the side of the parent they are presently with.

This may manifest in refusals to talk to the other parent on the phone or reluctance to share time with the other parent. Adolescents will typically act out in ways similar to how the parents are acting out.

In summary, expect that children will test a parent's loyalty, experience loyalty binds, not want to hurt either parent, force parents to interact because they don't want the divorce, try to exert some power in the situation, express anger over the divorce, occasionally refuse to go with the other parent (normal divorce stress, loyalty conflict/triangulation, or they may simply not want to stop doing what they're doing at the moment--similar to the reaction we've all gotten when we pick our children up from child care, or we want to go home from the park).

The most common problem which arise tend to stem from triangulation, divided loyalties, and projection. Some indicators of each are:

Chapter 1 - Living in Denial of your Divorce

a. Triangulation: Child refuses to have time with the other parent or talk to the other parent on the phone, child badmouths the other parent.

b. Divided loyalties: When a child tells each parent different and opposing things about what they want it is a good indication that the child is trying to please both parents and is experiencing divided loyalties.

c. Projection: Children are barometers of a parent's emotional well-being. Usually a parent reporting the stress of a child can not see that the child is acting on the parent's anxiety. Parents should ask themselves how they are feeling about the divorce, the other parent, and the time sharing arrangements before assuming the child is having difficulty adjusting or assuming the problem is with the other household.

Signs of Stress in Children

Sometimes parents need help identifying stress in children, especially little ones. What follows are some typical experiences and signs of stress in children of different ages.

I. INFANTS AND TODDLERS:

A. Regression in terms of sleeping, toilet training, or eating; slowing down in the mastery of new skills

B. Sleep disturbances *(difficulty going to sleep; frequent waking)*

C. Difficulty leaving parent; clinginess

D. General crankiness, temper tantrums, crying.

II. THREE TO FIVE YEARS:

A. Regression: returning to security blankets and discarded toys, lapses in toilet training, thumb sucking

B. Immature grasp of what has happened; bewildered; making up fantasy stories

C. Blaming themselves and feeling guilty

D. Bedtime anxiety; fitful/fretful sleep; frequent waking

E. Fear of being abandoned by both parents; clinginess

F. Greater irritability, aggression, temper tantrums.

III. SIX TO EIGHT YEARS:

A. Pervasive sadness; feeling abandoned and rejected

B. Crying and sobbing

C. Afraid of their worst fears coming true

D. Reconciliation fantasies

E. Loyalty conflicts; feeling physically torn apart

F. Problems with impulse control; disorganized behavior.

IV. NINE TO TWELVE YEARS:

A. Able to see family disruption clearly; try to bring order to situation

B. Fear of loneliness

C. Intense anger at the parent they blame for causing the divorce

D. Physical complaints; headaches and stomach aches

E. May become overactive to avoid thinking about the divorce

F. Feel ashamed of what's happening in their family; feel they are different from other children.

V. ADOLESCENTS:

A. Fear of being isolated and lonely

B. Experience parents as leaving them; feel parents are not available to them

C. Feel hurried to achieve independence

D. Feel in competition with parents

E. Worry about their own future loves and marriage; preoccupied with the survival of relationships

F. Discomfort with a parent's dating and sexuality

G. Chronic fatigue; difficulty concentrating

H. Mourn the loss of the family of their childhood.

CHAPTER 2
Rebuilding your Life After Divorce

"And the Lord God said, It is not good that the man should be alone; I will make him an help meet for him." **Genesis 2:18**

"For if they fall, the one will lift up his fellow: but woe to him that is alone when he falleth; for he hath not another to help him up." **Eccl 4:10**

The fact that you got divorce does not mean that you cannot enjoy life again. It is written, *"For a just man falleth seven times, and riseth up again: but the wicked shall fall into mischief."* **Proverb 24:16**

"Nothing is impossible with God." If your relationship failed you were responsible not God. God cannot not fail you if you whole heartedly trust in Him. Everyone is accountable for any failed marriage.

The one million dollar question is *what did I do wrong for my marriage to crash? Or was I in the right relationship in the first place?*

Although divorce can be complicated, it is one of the most complex emotional issues in relationship that can affect anyone. Often we do not seem to agree to the truth, but it takes a long time to recover from the emotional damages of divorce.

The best metaphor to qualify a divorce is like when there is death in the family. Adrenaline of sorrows, fear, anger, resentment, frustration, blame, fear, anguish, bitterness, hatred, and regret all kicks in at once.

Often the victim enters a mood of acceptance. They begin to worry and think. They start raising unanswerable questions that attached value to their self-worth and self-esteem. They enter into a lone judgmental phase where they will propound on every available choice *"If only I had done this..."* or *"I should have done this ..."* or *"I am not lovable"* or *"I'll never be happy"* or *"I'll always be alone."*

Chapter 2 - Rebuilding your Life after Divorce

Divorce can destroy anyone's self-esteem. Stress and depression can leave a permanent damage in the life of anyone who is not strong enough. Most couples go almost insane during the up and downs of the divorce process.

I love for you to understand that all those feelings and emotions are normal. We must embrace them instead of rejecting that they exist. Divorce can happen to the best woman and the best man on earth. We must embrace challenges as they come into our lives. That is why we are humans.

In life you will always be opposed by challenges. *"There hath no temptation taken you but such as is common to man: but God is faithful, who will not suffer you to be tempted above that ye are able; but will with the temptation also make a way to escape, that ye may be able to bear it."* **1cor10:13**

Jesus said, *"These things I have spoken unto you, that in me ye might have peace. In the world ye shall have tribulation: but be of good cheer; I have overcome the world."* **John16:33**

"Again, if two lie together, then they have heat: but how can one be warm alone?" **Eccl 4:11**

"And if one prevail against him, two shall withstand him; and a threefold cord is not quickly broken." **Eccl 4:12**

Divorce has never been easy for the couples involved, especially if they have children, real estate, and finances together.

It has a lasting effect on any new relationships. Often people let the frustration, and nightmare from their previous divorce to affect their new relationship.

Divorce is a learning experience that makes us stronger and healthier emotionally. It grants us faith, hope, and courage in the face of great disappointment and discouragement.

We are totally responsible for the outcome and how we act after our divorce. We can chose to become an angry person, a sad woman, or a depressed man. The truth is, the way you come out from any divorce is a determinant of your future relationship.

Chapter 2 - Rebuilding your Life after Divorce

Feelings of insecurity, betrayal, low self-esteem, and disconnection can linger long after a divorce. You could go through life blaming others for your unhappiness or you could choose to live and learn from this chapter of your life and rebuild your life.

Did You Survive a Divorce?

A divorce can be very devastating, it can be tumultuous time of financial, physical, spiritual, and emotional strain. Prevailing feelings of resentment, bitterness, hatred, rejection, loneliness, financial loss all play a pivotal role in altering the circumstances of our lives.

A lot of people have survived quiet a number of bitter divorce in the face of detrimental circumstances. A lot of others have lost their lives as a result of divorce. I do not know the present situation of your circumstance, but I do believe that you picked this small book for a genuine reason. May God deliver you from any forces raging against your marriage in the Mighty Name of Jesus.

I believe just about everyone can rebuild their life and live a happy life after a brutal divorce. It is all up to you. The fact that you got divorce does not stop your professional career from advancement, neither does it stop you from reaching your maximal potential in life.

He or she might not have been the best personality for you to relate with. There is someone for you out there. Or perhaps you neglected him or her. Everyone should be equally respected, cherished, and loved. I believe is will be nice and respectful if you stop loving anyone to let them know in the best way that they can understand you. Life I say all the time is what you make out of it.

To live a happy life or a miserable life depends on us. The bible says as a man thinks, so is he. Your personality attitude and the way you react and see others around you all play a vital role in your life. No man or woman is an island. *"And the Lord God said, It is not good that the man should be alone; I will make him an help meet for him."*

Chapter 2 - Rebuilding your Life after Divorce

There is someone out there for you. Have you found them respect, love, and cherish them in your life. *Are you still looking for them, then, pray for God to send the right person into your life?*

What I am saying is that you can rebuild your life. There is a great future awaiting for you. No man can stop you but you. God is not interested in your past. God want you to take advantage of your present condition, accept the realities in your life, and strive for a great future. I see you succeed in overcoming the memories of your divorce. I see you overcoming loneliness. I see you moving forward. I see you doing great things for the kingdom of God. I see you giving a great testimony in Jesus Name. Amen

CONCLUSION

"And the Lord God said, It is not good that the man should be alone; I will make him an help meet for him." **Genesis 2:18**

"For the Lord, the God of Israel, saith that he hateth putting away: for one covereth violence with his garment, saith the Lord of hosts: therefore take heed to your spirit, that ye deal not treacherously." **Mal 2:16**

Although God hates divorce, marriage is a good thing ordained by the Lord. No one can join themselves together and last in the relationship unless God join you together.

It is written, *"And said, For this cause shall a man leave father and mother, and shall cleave to his wife: and they twain shall be one flesh? Wherefore they are no more twain, but one flesh. What therefore God hath joined together, let not man put asunder."* **Mathew 19:5-6**.

Chapter 2 - Rebuilding your Life after Divorce

I pray you let God lead you to find your God ordained spouse in life.

"Therefore if any man be in Christ, he is a new creature: old things are passed away; behold, all things are become new." **2cor5:17**

It is written,
"But to the rest speak I, not the Lord: If any brother hath a wife that believeth not, and she be pleased to dwell with him, let him not put her away. And the woman which hath an husband that believeth not, and if he be pleased to dwell with her, let her not leave him. For the unbelieving husband is sanctified by the wife, and the unbelieving wife is sanctified by the husband: else were your children unclean; but now are they holy. But if the unbelieving depart, let him depart. A brother or a sister is not under bondage in such cases: but God hath called us to peace. For what knowest thou, O wife, whether thou shalt save thy husband? or how knowest thou, O man, whether thou shalt save thy wife?"
1cor7:12-16.

You must genuinely embrace the Lord Jesus. Righteousness has the power to vindicate anyone from any marital challenge in life. If you are genuinely born again help your spouse to become a genuine Christian also. The word says The Pharisees also came unto him, tempting him, and saying unto him, Is it lawful for a man to put away his wife for every cause?

"And he answered and said unto them, Have ye not read, that he which made them at the beginning made them male and female." **Mathew 19:4-5**

What must I do to determine my divine visitation?

To determine divine visitation you must be born again. The word says as many as received him, to them gave He power to become the sons of God. Even to them that believe on his name.

To qualify for divine visitation do the following sincerely;

1) Acknowledge that you are a sinner and that He died for you. **Rom3:23**.

2) Repent of your sins. **Acts 3:19, Luke13:5, 2Peter3:9**

3) Believe in your heart that Jesus died for your sin. **Romans10:10**

4) Confess Jesus as the Lord over your life. **Romans10:10, Acts2:21**

Chapter 2 - Rebuilding your Life after Divorce

Now repeat this Prayer after me

Say Lord Jesus, I accept you today, as my Lord and my savior, forgive me of my sins wash me with your blood. Right now, I believe, I am sanctified, I am save, I am free, I am free from the Power of sin to serve the Lord Jesus. Thank you Lord for saving me. Amen.

I adjure you to watch the Spirit of God bear witness with your Spirit confirming His word with signs following. The word says The Spirit itself beareth witness with our spirit, that we are the children of God. Join a bible believing church or join us on our weekly and Sunday worship services at 343 Sanford Avenue Newark New Jersey 07106.

WISDOM KEYS

Every Productive Society is a society heading to the top

Millions of Nigerians run away from Nigeria, very few Nigerians stay in Nigeria.

My decision to return Nigeria is the will of God for my life

My short coming in America after 18 years, trained me to be wise, to think, reflect and reason appropriately.

If you train your mind to reason it will train your hands to earn money.

It is absurd to use the money of the heathen to build the kingdom of the living God.

Every Ministry reveals its agenda and goal either at the beginning or at the end. Be careful of your life it is your first Ministry.

The average American mind is conditioned for a continual quest to get new things and (discard the former) and throw away old things.

Chapter 2 - Rebuilding your Life after Divorce

When I considered well, my BMW jeep became my initial deposit for the work of the ministry in Nigeria

Everyone is waiting for you to change your mind until you change your thinking nothing changes around you.

Multiple academic degrees in other discipline gave me the chance to think, reflect and reason

What so everyone are thinking and reflecting at the moment reveals you to the time and the now factor

All events and intents are the product of precise thought processes, accurate reason every event is designed for a designated timeline

Wisdom is your ability to think, to create and invent. If you can think wise enough you will come out of penury

The distance between you and success is your creative ability to think reason and reflect accurate.

Success is the result of hard work, commitment resolve and determination learning from past mistakes and failing.

If you organize your mind you have organized your life and destiny.

There is a thin line between success and failure. If you look above and beyond you are on your way to success.

Wealth is your ability to think, power is your ability to reason and success is your ability to be informed.

If you can make use of your mind by thinking and reasoning God will make use of your life and destiny.

Think and Be Great

Reflect, Reason, think and be great

Famous people are born of woman

Chapter 2 - Rebuilding your Life after Divorce

That you will make it is your intention; that you will survive is your resolve, that you will succeed with changes is your determination, personal efforts and hard work.

No man was born a failure. Lack of vision is the end product of failure.

Working with mental patients encourages and aspire me to be a productive observant and dedicated to my assignment.

Successful people are not magicians, it is the will power combined with hard work, and determination and a resolve to succeed that make them succeed.

In the unequivocal state of the mind, intention is not a location or a position it is the state of the mind.

So many people think that they think. The mind is used to think reflect and reason. You will remain blind with your eye open until you can see with your mind by thinking.

There is no favoritism in accurate and precise calculation

Although knowledge is power, information is the key and gateway to a great future.

It will take the hand of God to move the hand of man.

With the backing of the great wise God, nothing will disconnect you from your inheritance.

As long as you have wisdom and understanding of God, Satan and evil cannot manipulate your life and destiny.

You have come this far by yourself judgment and decision you have made in the past, now lean and listen to God for another dimension of greatness.

Great people are common people it is extra ordinary effort and the price of sacrifice that produces greatness.

As a mental direct care worker I saw a great pastor and a motivational speaker within myself.

Menial job does not reduce your self-worth, until you resolve to achieve greatness see greatness in all you do; you will never count in your community

Chapter 2 - Rebuilding your Life after Divorce

The principle of Jesus will solve your gambling and addiction problems

The man of Jesus will lead you into heaven,

Everyone have their self-appraisal and what they think about you. Until you discover yourself other opinion about you will alter the real you.

Supervisors and directors are just a position in the chain of command in a work place. Never allow your supervisor hierarchy to alter your opinion about yourself.

Everyone can come out of debt if they make up their mind.

That I am not a decision maker at work does not diminish my contribution to my world.

Although it appears like it was a poor decision to accept a direct care employment at a psychiatric hospital as I reflect of my nine years of experience, it became apparent that I have learnt and experienced enough for my next assignment.

Self-encouragement and determination is a resolve of the heart.

If you are determined to make a difference, and do the things that make a difference you will eventually make a difference.

Good things do not come easy

Short cuts will cut your life short.

Those who look ahead move ahead.

Life is all about making an impact. In your life time strive to make an impact in your community.

Make friends and connect with people who are moving ahead of you in life.

If you can look around well you have come a long way in your life, made a lot of difference and realized a lot of success in life.

If you are my old friend, hurry up to reach out to me before I become a stranger to you.

Everything I am blessed with inspirations from God, that change my definition and interpretation of the world around me.

I thought I was stagnant and lonely until I looked around and noticed my children running around and my wife cooking.

Chapter 2 - Rebuilding your Life after Divorce

At 40 I resigned my Job to seek the Lord forever.

My ministry took a drastic rise to the top when the wisdom of God visited me with knowledge and understanding.

You will be a better person if you understand the characteristics of your personality – your mood swings attitudes and habits.

It is the seed of love you sow into the heart of a child and a woman that you reap in due time.

Love is not selfish, love share everything including the concealed secrets of the mind.

As long as you have a prayer life and a bible; you will never feel lonely, rejected and idle in the race of life.

When good friends disconnect from you, let them go, they might have seen something new in a different direction.

Confidence in yourself and in God is the only way to bring you out of captivity

Never train a child to waste his/her time.

The mind is the greatest assets of a great future.

You walk by common sense run by principles and fly by instruction.

Those who fly in flight of life fly alone.

Up in the air you are alone. No one can toll you accept the compass of knowledge and information

I have seen a tolling vehicle I have seen a tolling ship I have never seen a tolling airplane.

I exercise my judgment and make a decision every minute of the day.

Decisions are crucial, critical and vital with reference to your future.

So many people wish for a great future. You can only work towards a great future.

Your celebrity status began when you discovered your talent. What are you good at? Work at it with all commitment.

Prayers will sustain you but the wisdom of God will prosper you.

When I met Oyedepo, his teachings changed my perspective, but when I met Ibiyeomie; His teaching changed my perception.

I will be successful in ministry if only I concentrate and focus my energy in the work of the ministry.

It took the late Dr. Vincent Pearle Norman's book to open my mind towards kingdom success.

CHAPTER 3
PRAYER OF SALVATION

"Neither is there salvation in any other: for there is none other name under heaven given among men, whereby we must be saved." **Acts4:12**

One of the reasons we suffer bitterness, hatred and rejection is because we do not know the power in the Name of Jesus. I want you to consciously take the Name of Jesus serious in your life. Believe in that name. It will deliver you from relationship nightmares, and bitterness.

The word of God says *"The name of the Lord is a strong tower: the righteous runneth into it, and is safe."* **Proverb18:10**

Are you saved?

To be saved we must be born again!

The word says as many as received him, to them gave He power to become the sons of God. Even to them that believe on his name.

To qualify for divine visitation do the following sincerely,

1) Acknowledge that you are a sinner and that He died for you. **Rom3:23.**

2) Repent of your sins. **Acts 3:19, Luke13:5, 2Peter3:9**

3) Believe in your heart that Jesus died for your sin. **Romans10:10**

4) Confess Jesus as the Lord over your life. **Romans10:10, Acts2:21**

Now repeat this Prayer after me

Say Lord Jesus, I accept you today, as my Lord and my savior, forgive me of my sins wash me with your blood. Right now, I believe, I am sanctified, I am save, I am free, I am free from the Power of sin to serve the Lord Jesus. Thank you Lord for saving me. Amen.

I adjure you to watch the Spirit of God bear witness with your Spirit confirming His word with signs following. The word says The Spirit itself beareth witness with our spirit, that we are the children of God.

Chapter 3 - Prayer of Salvation

MIRACLE CARE OUTREACH

"...But that the members should have the same care one for another" **1cor12:25**

We are all members of the body of Christ. Jesus commanded us to love our neighbor as ourselves. This includes caring for one another as a member of one body. True love is expressed in caring and giving. The word says for God so Love He gave….

Reach out to someone in need of Jesus, help someone in crisis find Christ. Look out and prove your love to Jesus by caring and inviting your friends and associates to find Jesus the Healer.

Invite your friends to our Home Care Cell Fellowship (Miracle chapel Intl Satellite fellowship) In the USA at 33 Schley Street Newark New Jersey 07112.

If you are in Nigeria—**MIRACLE OF GOD MINISTRIES**

A.K.A "MIRACLE CHAPEL INTL" Mpama –Egbu-Owerri Imo state Nigeria.

(Home Care Cell fellowship Group). We meet every Tuesday at 6:00pm-7:00pm.

LIFE IS NOT ALL ABOUT DURATION BUT ITS ALL ABOUT DONATION

What does the above statement mean?....

"Life consists not in accumulation of material wealth.." **Luke12:15.**

"But it's all about liberality....meaning- what you can give and share with others." **Proverb11:25.**

When you live for others--You live forever- because you out live your generation by the legacy you live behind after you depart into glory to be with the Lord. But when you live to yourself - you are reduced to self—you are easily forgotten when you die and depart in glory.

Permit me to admonish you today to live your life to be a blessing to a soul connected to you today.

Chapter 3 - Prayer of Salvation

I want you to know that so many souls are connected and looking up to you, and through you so many souls will be saved and rescued from destruction. Will you disciple someone today to find Jesus Christ?

"As a genuine Christian; it is your duty to evangelize Jesus Christ to all you meet on your way. Jesus is still in the healing business-Jesus is still doing miracles from time of old to now.

Therefore tell someone about Jesus Christ today, disciple and bring them to Church."

John 1:45 Philip findeth Nathanael....

Please to prove the sincerity of your love for God today; please become a soul winner. The dignity of your Christianity is hidden in your boldness to proclaim and evangelize Jesus Christ to all you meet on your way.

There is a question mark on the integrity of your Christianity until you become a life soul winner. Invite someone to join us worship the Lord Jesus this coming Sunday.

MIRACLE OF GOD MINISTRIES

PILLARS OF THE COMMISSION

We Believe Preach and Practice the following,

1) We believe and preach Salvation to every living human being

2) We believe and preach Repentance and forgiveness of sins

3) We believe and preach the baptism of the Holy Spirit and Spiritual gifts

4) We believe and teach the Prosperity

5) We believe and preach Divine Healing and Miracles (Signs &Wonder)

6) We believe and preach Faith

7) We believe and Proclaim the Power of God (Supernatural)

8) We believe and Proclaim Praise& Worship to God

9) We believe and preach Wisdom

10) We believe and preach Holiness (Consecration)

11) We believe and preach Vision

12) We believe and teach the Word of God

13) We believe and teach Success

14) We believe and practice Prayer

15) We believe and teach Deliverance

This 15 stones form the Pillars of Our Commission.

Become part of this church family and follow this great move of God.

MY HEART FELT PRAYER FOR YOU

It is my prayer that you testify today about the goodness of the Lord. I desire for you to overcome the memory of any divorce if any in your life in the mighty name of Jesus Christ.

Now let me Pray for you:

Lord Jesus, I give you thanks and praise. Father bring joy, peace, and happiness in the life of this precious love one reading this small book. If they have suffered the nightmare, and bitterness of divorce, Father grant them peace of the heart. I thank you for giving them another chance to build a lasting relationship in Jesus Mighty Name.

Amen.

CHAPTER 4
ABOUT THE AUTHOR

Rev Franklin N Abazie is the founding and Presiding Pastor of Miracle of God Ministries with headquarters in Newark, New Jersey USA and a branch church in Owerri- Imo State Nigeria. He is following the footsteps of one of his mentors, Oral Roberts (Healing Evangelist) of the blessed memory.

The Lord passed Oral Roberts healing mantle two days before he went to be with the Lord at age 91 into the hand of healing evangelist-Rev Franklin N Abazie in a vision.

In all his services the Power and Presence of God is present to heal all in his audience. He is an ordained man of God with a Healing Ministry reviving the healing and miracle ministry of Jesus Christ of Nazareth.

Pastor Franklin N Abazie, is called by God with a unique mandate:

"THE MOMENT IS DUE TO IMPACT YOUR WORLD THROUGH THE REVIVAL OF THE HEALING & MIRACLE MINISTRY OF JESUS CHRIST OF NAZARETH.

I AM SENDING YOU TO RESTORE HEALTH UNTO THEE AND I WILL HEAL THEE OF THY WOUNDS. SAID THE LORD OF HOST"

He is a gifted ardent Teacher of the word of God who operates also in the office of a Prophet, generating and attracting undeniable signs & wonders, special miracles and healings, with apostolic fireworks of the Holy Ghost.

He is the founding and presiding senior Pastor of this fast growing Healing ministry.

He has written over 86 inspirational, healing and transforming books covering almost all aspect of divine healing and life. He is happily married and blessed with children.

BOOKS BY REV FRANKLIN N ABAZIE

1) Commanding Abundance
2) The outcome of faith
3) Understanding the secret of prevailing prayers
4) Understanding the secret of the man God uses
5) Activating my due Season
6) Overcoming Divine Verdicts
7) The Outcome of Divine Wisdom
8) Understanding God's Restoration Mandate
9) Walking in the Victory and Authority of the truth
10) Gods Covenant Exemption
11) Destiny Restoration Pillars
12) Provoking Acceptable Praise
13) Understanding Divine Judgment
14) Activating Angelic Re-enforcement
15) Provoking Un-Merited Favor
16) The Benefits of the Speaking faith
17) Understanding Divine Arrangement

18) Understanding Divine Healing
19) The Mystery of Endurance
20) Obeying Divine Instructions
21) Understanding the Voice of God
22) Never give up on Hope
23) The prevailing Power of faith
24) Understanding Divine Prosperity
25) The Reward of Prayer
26) Covenant Keys to Answered Prayers
27) Activating the Forces of Vengeance
28) Put your faith to work
29) Where is your trust?
30) The Audacity of the Blood of Jesus
31) Redeeming Your Days
32) The force of Vision
33) Breaking the shackles of Family Curses
34) Wisdom for Marriage Stability
35) Overcoming prevailing challenges
36) The Prayer solution
37) The power of Prayer
38) The Effective Strategy of Prayer
39) The prayer that works
40) Walking in Forgiveness
41) The power of the grace of God

42) The Power of Persistence
43) Overcoming Divine verdicts
44) The audacity of the blood of Jesus.
45) The prevailing power of the blood of Jesus
46) The benefit of the speaking faith.
47) Fearless faith
48) Redeeming Your Days.
49) The Supernatural Power of Prophecy
50) The companionship of the Holy Spirit
51) Understanding Divine Judgement
52) Understanding Divine Prosperity
53) Dominating Controlling Forces
54) The winners Faith
55) Destiny Restoration Pillars
56) Developing Spiritual Muscles
57) Inexplicable faith
58) The lifestyle of Prayer
59) Developing a positive attitude in life.
60) The mystery of Divine supply
61) Encounter with the Power of God
62) Walking in love
63) Praying in the Spirit
64) How to provoke your testimony

65) Walking in the reality of the Anointing
66) The reality of new birth
67) The price of freedom
68) The Supernatural power of faith
69) The intellectual components of Redemption
70) Overcoming Fear
71) Overcoming Prevailing Challenges
72) My life & Ministry
73) The Mystery of Praise

MIRACLE OF GOD MINISTRIES

NIGERIA CRUSADE 2012

MIRACLE OF GOD MINISTRIES
NIGERIA CRUSADE 2012

MIRACLE OF GOD MINISTRIES

NIGERIA CRUSADE

2012

MIRACLE OF GOD MINISTRIES

NIGERIA CRUSADE

2012

www.ingramcontent.com/pod-product-compliance
Lightning Source LLC
Chambersburg PA
CBHW020035120526
44588CB00031B/705